TABLE OF CONTENTS

Page

ACRONYMS

CGSC	Command and General Staff College
CSA	Chief of Staff, United States Army
ICRC	International Committee of the Red Cross
IDF	Israel Defense Forces
IMF	International Monetary Fund
MMAS	Master of Military Art and Science
NATO	North Atlantic Treaty Organization
SAMS	School of Advanced Military Studies
TTPs	Tactics, Techniques and Procedures

CHAPTER 1

INTRODUCTION

The ever-increasing presence of social media throughout the world requires military members to be cognizant of their actions at all times. In contrast to the news crews traditional media heretofore brought to areas in which militaries operate, "social media" can literally consist of anyone in the world with a camera phone and access to the Internet. To address this significant cultural change, I offer a framework for military operations which includes social media as a primary consideration. In particular, I describe critical aspects of the Egyptian Army's response to the so-called Arab Spring as a way of illustrating how militaries may respond to popular movements. Utilizing the unique oral history of a company commander who led soldiers in Cairo's Tahrir Square throughout the events of 2011, I examine the Egyptian response in light of my proposed framework. Ultimately, I argue that the Egyptian Army's experiences in 2011 provide a powerful example of how militaries may think about social media as a factor in military operations.

To arrive at this thesis, however, it is first necessary to describe the motivation behind this research, along with the significance of the study, limitations, strengths, and operational definitions to be used throughout the paper. This chapter describes these background elements, while succeeding chapters proceed as follows: chapter 2 contains a comprehensive review of the existing literature on transformative social movements, social media, and the widespread popular movement collectively known as the Arab Spring. The paper recapitulates work in these key areas to reveal a gap in literature, which does not adequately contemplate the military perspective of social media throughout the events of early 2011. It also characterizes the void in scholarship originating from military professionals who are often reluctant to engage scholars with regard to actual events in which they have participated. This reluctance increases the extant gap in scholarly coverage of the Egyptian Army's response to its national crisis. Chapter 2 addresses the extent to which Egyptian forces were affected by how they were portrayed in social media platforms in Tahrir Square[1] in 2011, eventually arriving at the key research question outlined in chapter 1—namely, how should militaries think about social media as a factor in their operations?

Chapter 3 describes the methodology I utilize, which emphasizes the unique oral history of an Egyptian company commander who led soldiers in Tahrir Square throughout several months of intensive security operations[2] during the Arab Spring. By focusing on this key individual during the most critical time and location within the Arab Spring, the paper serves as a descriptive study. In turn, this study enables my proposal of a theoretical framework to understand the effects of social media on militaries. In chapter 4, I describe fully this framework, based on Gene Sharp's pamphlet on nonviolent resistance,[3] and evaluate findings of this study through the lens of my proposed

---

[1]"Cairo's Tahrir Square is justifiably perceived as the symbolic heart of the '25 January Revolution.'" Amnesty International, *Egypt Rises: Killings, Detentions and torture in the 25 January Revolution* (London: Amnesty International Ltd., 2011), 30.

[2]I define these operations as being concerned with "maintenance of public order and security. ICRC.org, "Police and Security Forces," International Committee of the Red Cross (ICRC) Resource Center, http://www.icrc.org/eng/resources/documents/misc/57jq3h.htm (accessed 31 May 2012), chapter 1, sub-part B below.

[3]See chapters 2 and 4 for thorough discussions of this seminal work.

framework. The use of specific examples from the Egyptian case study permits me to arrive at a useful answer to my central research question.

I find the prevalence of social media significantly affected the Egyptian Army's response to the massive 2011 popular uprising. I suggest that a useful way to think about social media in military operations is to examine the Egyptian Army approach in light of the updated Sharp framework. The introduction of Gene Sharp's principles adds to an understanding of what the protestors in Tahrir Square sought to achieve; it follows that a similar understanding will inform the way military professionals respond to similar events in the future. Further, I argue that a written account of the Egyptian Army's response to social media is exactly the type of "policy-relevant scholarship" military practitioners must be willing to produce in order to inform U.S. policy in a truly meaningful way. Finally, in chapter 5, I share discoveries that emerged during the course of this study, describe the significance of my conclusions, and make recommendations for future research in this critically important area affecting militaries throughout the world.

We Are the Egyptian Army-Background

In January 2011, President Hosni Mubarak ordered the Egyptian Army to respond to massive demonstrations occurring throughout Egypt.[4] Military officers were tasked with securing key areas during this high-visibility event capable of escalating into armed

---

[4]The catalyst for the Arab Spring revolution in Egypt is widely regarded as a Facebook page, set up by Google executive Wael Ghonim, entitled "We Are All Khaled Said." Ghonim established this page in memory of Said, an individual allegedly tortured and killed by Egyptian police for uploading a police corruption video on YouTube (Eric Harr, "The Real Truth about Social Media" (Campbell, CA: FastPencil, Inc., 2011), xxiii-xxiv.

conflict. Popular uprisings had occurred in major cities throughout Egypt, with the crowds' ostensible intention being not only to increase the Egyptian Government's accountability for its increasingly authoritarian actions, but also to immediately remove Mubarak from office. The crowds grew to over one million in Cairo's Tahrir Square, specifically, and over one million in several other Egyptian cities, as that nation's contribution to the "Arab Spring" of 2011 became apparent.[5] To a large extent, the mass gatherings were the direct result of Facebook pages (and Twitter feeds) designed to rally individuals to particular times and places to protest the government en masse. Put simply, government officials—including the president—in Egypt were about to be "ousted due to mass protests coordinated and announced through social media" (Thompson 2011, 175). Shutting off Internet connectivity and cell phone service did not help the Egyptian Government's efforts,[6] as doing so actually caused more people to leave their residences and join the crowd, particularly in Cairo's Tahrir Square (Egyptian Army Officer 2012).[7] In response to the massive crowds, which overwhelmed the Egyptian police forces, the government called upon its Army to secure critical areas and prevent the spread of

---

[5]The massive gatherings in Egypt occurred over the course of eighteen days, from 25 January 2011, through 11 February 2011, though military forces remain in key areas throughout Egypt at the time of this writing.

[6]It also did not help the Egyptian Army's efforts, given that cell phones serve as the primary means of direct communication between tactical and operational level commanders. Egyptian Army Officer, interview by author, Ft. Leavenworth, KS, 27 March 2012. See also Amnesty International, 21.

[7]Perhaps this is because people had nothing better to do without Internet connectivity. Thus, while social media certainly accelerated the movement, it did not necessarily cause every individual who participated in the uprising to decide to do so (though the "absence of social media" during the time without Internet connectivity may therefore be described as a cause).

violence. Calling in the military worked, as Egyptian forces met this intent and generally reduced the potential for violence by taking control of the situation.

The Egyptian Army, in its belief that it maintained more credibility than the president with the people at that critical moment, knew it had to act in a way to reduce violence and chaos (Egyptian Army Officer 2012). Moreover, Egypt's concern for the international public's perception of its Army led directly to several critical decisions: first, the decision to remove lethal ammunition from all soldiers' weapons; second, the decision to approve soldiers' posing for Facebook photos on military equipment with protesters (Egyptian Army Officer 2012); third, a decision not to require a curfew of citizens in Tahrir Square, in contrast with virtually all other gathering areas, for which curfews were imposed in order to reduce the likelihood of violence. These three particular decisions undoubtedly left the Army more vulnerable in terms of safety, firepower, and the ability to control the situation, were it to get out of hand. Yet, the military leadership felt these steps were essential to de-escalate the situation, particularly in the city of Cairo. Soon thereafter, Egyptian Army leadership made a fourth important decision—involving the tacit approval of soldiers' ability to publicly respond to misinformation, in contravention of strict Egyptian policy ordinarily preventing such public discourse by military members—designed to mitigate the speed with which inflammatory, anti-military information might spread throughout the nation. Why would the Egyptian military come to these conclusions? Did the prevalence of social media cause, or contribute significantly, to these conclusions? These are questions I seek to answer throughout this work.

Given the fascinating events much of the world's population watched live on various media platforms, it becomes worthwhile to more closely examine aspects of the military response—one which ultimately reduced tensions and calmed the nation within a matter of days. The potential causes of the uprising across the Middle East, and Egypt in particular, are covered in various studies throughout the past year in an interesting and thought-provoking manner.[8] This paper, however, is more concerned with the social media aspects of the uprising, to include the use of Facebook and Twitter, along with—as events further developed—camera phones at actual protests throughout the most intensive (initial) phase of the revolution.

While considering the significance of the widely viewed events in Egypt, I happened upon a unique opportunity—one which ultimately would become highly relevant to my interest in determining how the U.S. military may respond to increasingly prevalent social movements and the massive uprisings they may engender. Specifically, I had the fortune of working directly with an Egyptian Army Officer who had served as one of the few company commanders in Cairo's Tahrir Square throughout the Arab Spring. In fact, this Army major[9] led soldiers from the day the Egyptian military arrived in Tahrir Square until virtually the day I met him several months thereafter. Returning to my previous characterization of Egyptian Army leadership, it is certainly reasonable to

---

[8]See chapter 2's Literature Review for detailed coverage of these publications.

[9]Out of an abundance of caution, I do not identify this individual by name throughout this work. Not wanting to risk his personal security in any way, I will simply reiterate the fact that this officer led soldiers in Tahrir Square every day from the beginning of the Egyptian "Arab Spring" until virtually the day I met him—a span of several months literally on the front lines of this nation-changing event.

include this company commander as an integral part of that group of most important decision makers immediately involved in the response to this uprising.

Operational Definitions

Importantly, as an operational definition of 'social media,' I include Facebook, Twitter, YouTube, and social networking sites not specifically named but potentially used in the events described throughout the paper. I also include camera phone images and videos under the rubric of social media throughout the work, since the widespread effect of such images and videos is truly realized only when they are uploaded and disseminated through the aforementioned social networking sites.

As an operational definition of 'security operations' for the purposes of this paper, I use the International Committee of the Red Cross (ICRC) standard of "maintenance of public order and security" (ICRC 2012). The ICRC definition of security operations is valuable for two reasons. First, because of the pre-eminence typically afforded the ICRC in the international community, ICRC definitions in matters of international security and conflicts studies may be viewed as authoritative. Second, the conflation of 'security operations' with 'maintenance of public order and security' in the ICRC definition is highly useful for describing a situation in which public order and security are equally paramount, as they were in Tahrir Square and throughout Egypt during the Arab Spring timeframe.

Limitations

One challenge of this type of project is the relative lack of literature on the subject. Though a significant amount of work exists to discuss the effects of social media in today's society, the recent (and, in many ways, still developing) nature of the events of the Arab Spring serve as a limitation on the completeness of the study. For example, as of the writing of this thesis, the Egyptian Army continues to maintain a presence in Tahrir Square (Egyptian Army Officer 2012). Therefore, complete data in political science terms is not available as of this writing. Nevertheless, the extremely recent nature of events within this particular topic can strengthen the work, as well. For example, the relevance and timeliness of social media literature to date, as described in chapter 2, assists militaries in knowing exactly what they may face in terms of technology on the battlefield in the near-term future.

Another limitation is the inability of the study to represent more than one Egyptian Army company commander's worth of perspective on the events in Cairo in 2011. This challenge is described in chapter 3 (methodology), and underscores the categorization of this research as a "descriptive study." This potential drawback is often characterized statistically as an "N=1" study, given the use of one main subject as a data set. However, as I argue in chapter 3, this limitation is strongly mitigated by the ability to describe with great detail the Egyptian Army's perspective of social media in Tahrir Square. Even with an "N=1," the study succeeds as a direct result of the ability to introduce a new concept from which other similarly situated individuals may learn. To be exact, anecdotal evidence from this Egyptian company commander's leadership experiences during an unprecedented event gives a clear understanding of how social media may accelerate popular movements. Such unique and valuable experience qualifies as a new concept from which other leaders and militaries may learn.

A final limitation on the ability to draw broad-based conclusions from this study is the decision to view the Arab Spring exclusively through the lens of the Egyptian experience, in general, and through the events of Tahrir Square, in particular. Thus, while the broadly-recognized term "Arab Spring" is used to describe the movement under which events in Egypt were known to occur, this work does not seek to generalize results from Egypt for universal application to all so-called Arab Spring countries.

Delimitations

While several related subjects are undoubtedly worth further inquiry, this study does not contemplate causes of the revolution, religious aspects of the revolution, the reach and use of Internet amongst youth in Egypt, or the actual content of Facebook and Twitter posts which made such a difference in the protests. The police response—or lack of response, as the case may be—to events in Egypt serves as another delimitation of the study, and would be a worthwhile subject for future research, as would any differences between groups within the crowd in terms of how much they sought to provoke an overreaction on behalf of the Egyptian Army.[10]

The extent to which the United States may have played a role in "fomenting protests" during the Arab Spring, by training protest leaders to "organiz[e] through new media tools" (Nixon 2011, 1), while relevant, is outside the scope of this particular

---

[10]It should also be noted that organizations such as Amnesty International have made allegations against the Egyptian police and military of harsh treatment toward 'innocent persons' throughout the time of the revolution. The validity of these allegations is also outside the scope of this work. For a complete discussion of these allegations. See Amnesty International, *Egypt Rises: Killings, Detentions and Torture in the 25 January Revolution* (London: Amnesty Interntaional Ltd., 2011).

work.[11] Finally, any discussion of recent popular movements in other societies, to include the so-called Occupy movements throughout the United States, and International Monetary Fund (IMF), G20, and North Atlantic Treaty Organization (NATO) Summit protests throughout the world, are not included in this study.

Significance of the Study

Notwithstanding the limitations described above, this project is significant for its contribution to the future of military security missions. Social media on the "battlefield"[12] will drastically affect soldiers' behavior, particularly given that militaries will increasingly be required to respond to transformative movements, mass demonstrations and uprisings throughout the world in the future. The ability to capture the actual, real-world perspective from an Egyptian commander in Tahrir Square during the uprising and aftermath represents a unique and significant contribution to the literature on this subject. While there does not appear to have been one specific cause for the Arab Spring, United States military (and civilian) leaders need to learn as much as possible about social movements, how to predict patterns of outcomes, and generally how

---

[11]As one example, "[s]tate-owned newspapers [in Egypt even] accused activists of receiving money from American intelligence agencies." Ron Nixon, "U.S. Groups Helped Nurture Arab Uprisings," *New York Times*, 15 April 2011, 3. At a minimum, according to the *New York Times*, it is clear that "[s]ome Egyptian youth leaders attended a 2008 technology meeting in New York, where they were taught to use social networking and mobile technologies to promote democracy. Among those sponsoring the meeting were Facebook, Google, MTV, Columbia Law School, and the State Department" (Nixon, 1).

[12]Wherever that term may apply. Again, a complete discussion of what constitutes a 'battlefield' in the contemporary fight is outside the scope of this paper.

to effectively deal with mass uprisings while serving in increasingly complex and interconnected environments.

Events in early 2011 in Egypt portend significant ramifications for how United States, and other, militaries perform future security missions. Because military actions are often viewed under a microscope, planning and decision making in transformative events such as those that occurred in Egypt are critical. It is precisely because of this reason that I argue that militaries will conduct key aspects of security missions differently out of fear for how they may be negatively portrayed in social media. Ultimately, my research question lies therein; namely, how to think about social media as a factor in military operations? As a related question, I ask the extent to which Egyptian Army forces were affected by how they were perceived by the public through social media platforms during the Arab Spring events in Cairo. How to arrive at the scholarly gap in which these questions reside is a matter which will be explored in depth in chapter 2. Before analyzing the value of this type of work, however, a review of the literature bringing us to this point is first necessary, and is a subject to which I will now turn.

CHAPTER 2

LITERATURE REVIEW

To understand how to think about social media as a factor in military operations, and the extent to which Egyptian Army forces were affected by how they were portrayed in social media platforms in Tahrir Square, it is first necessary to discuss previous literature on the subject. In fact, two main areas of study impact the events in Egypt. These areas include general social movement/social media theory, and specific Arab Spring literature, which centers largely on the ability of social media to unite and inspire population masses. Ultimately, a study of this literature reveals a gap, as discussion of the specific effect of social media on Egyptian Army forces during the 2011 revolution remains largely absent.

In response to scholarly forerunners in the above-described relevant areas, I arrive at a thesis not contemplated by previous work; namely, that the Egyptian Army's experience in early 2011 provides a powerful example of how militaries may think about social media as a factor in military operations. At a minimum, the Army acted differently than it otherwise would have, out of concern for how it may be negatively portrayed in social media during the Arab Spring. As described in chapter 4, Egyptian military leaders were very aware of the perception of their forces amongst Egyptian citizens and the world. As a result, they aggressively sought to ensure that the worldwide audience knew the Army was "there to protect" the millions of people in locations such as Cairo's Tahrir Square (Egyptian Army Officer 2012). This overwhelming desire to protect the citizenry led to a number of social media-related decisions on behalf of the Egyptian Army leadership. Though several more illustrations of this approach are described in chapter 4, two examples of these decisions include the removal of all live ammunition from weapons, avoiding any images or videos suggesting a heavy-handed Army approach, and a willingness to allow protestors to pose on military vehicles for camera phone photographs, reinforcing the notion of an Army protecting—and not intimidating—its citizenry.[13]

The question of how to think about social media as a factor in military operations drives the methodology described in chapter 3, as well as the in-depth analysis in chapter 4. To fill the gap that exists relating to the military's approach to social media during the Arab Spring, I propose a framework for analyzing "social media warfare"[14] in chapter 4. This framework updates a well-known theory on nonviolent resistance—Gene Sharp's "From Dictatorship to Democracy: A Conceptual Framework for Liberation"—to include social media considerations. By examining the Egyptian Army's approach to the events of 2011 in light of this updated Sharp framework, a useful way to think about social media in military operations emerges. Yet to fully understand this framework, it is necessary to first review the scholarship development up to and including the point in time at which the Egyptian Army confronted massive protestors armed with camera phones, Twitter feeds, and Facebook accounts.

<u>Social Movement/Social Media Theory</u>

To discuss the importance of social media as a factor in military operations, it is first necessary to briefly examine literature describing the willingness of individuals to

---

[13]See chapter 4 for a complete description and exact citation of these claims.

[14]This newly devised term is introduced and explained in chapter 4, sub-part B.

organize and engage within their societies. This literature begins with seminal works on social movements. Such theories begin to describe exactly what unites and inspires popular uprisings in order for social media platforms to both harness and accelerate these transformative events throughout various societies.

Gene Sharp's "From Dictatorship to Democracy: A Conceptual Framework for Liberation" is perhaps the dominant piece of literature in the area of leaderless social movements. Since its publication in 1993, Sharp's pamphlet, with a particular focus on non-violent resistance, has "arguably become *the* how-to guide to topple autocrats" (ISN 2012). Though published years before the events of the Arab Spring, the book's "methods have been influential in the toppling of Zine El Abidine Ben Ali in Tunisia, Hosni Mubarak in Egypt, and have also been used (in part) in Libya and Syria. Indeed, its use has prompted some commentators to speak of Gene Sharp as the Arab Spring's 'intellectual mastermind'" (ISN 2012).

I unpack the social media implications of Sharp's tactics for popular movements in chapter 4; however, two examples serve to illustrate the appropriateness of a study 'standing on the shoulders' of Sharp's giant contribution in this arena. First, Sharp's tactics include an "appeal to international audiences," which social media can and certainly did accomplish in the case of the Arab Spring (ISN 2012). Second, Sharp calls for a form of struggle with "social 'weapons' being used rather than military-industrial ones" (ISN 2012). Both the appeal to international audiences and the use of social weapons in Sharp's work are key aspects with which militaries must deal; it follows that knowledge of each, even from a narrow lens into the Egyptian Army's efforts in early 2011, contributes to both scholars' and practitioners' interests in this area.

Certain scholars offer further perspective in the area of leaderless social movements. These studies focus on the capabilities of groups to successfully organize, even without leadership. For example, in *The Leaderless Social Movement Organization: Unstoppable Power or Last-Ditch Effort*, Justin Hsu and Brian Low examine the conditions under which leaderless social movement organizations are more or less likely to be effective. They conclude that social movements are allowed more structured and centralized organization in states with a low capacity to repress them, whereas social movements are less likely to have centralized organization in states with a high capacity to repress their citizens (Hsu and Low 2010).

Social media literature amplifies and updates social movement theory in a meaningful way. Social media differs from traditional media in that, with social media, "anyone with a cell phone can become a reporter and take a cell phone video of news while it is happening" (Thompson 2011, 171). Yet before the existence of camera phones, Facebook, Twitter, and other social networking sites, individuals' behavior changed with the advent of the Internet. Early social media literature discusses the ability of technology to promote individualism and make it more difficult to govern and organize a coherent society (Pool 1990). In essence, this begins to explain the link between various social movements and social media. As Ithiel de Sola Pool describes in *Technologies Without Boundaries*, revolutions in communications technologies profoundly affect social life and culture (Pool 1990). Though Pool obviously had no knowledge of Facebook or other social media at the time of his writing, it is interesting to note the extent to which social media, a "revolution in communications technology" profoundly affects nearly all aspects of present-day social life and culture.

David Brin's compelling work in this arena centers on the ability of the Internet to serve as a "Disputation Arena," in which various parties can debate positions on critical matters (Brin 2000).[15] In his 2000 study, Brin argues that individuals "need secure enclaves to gather allies, make plans, and prepare for coming battles" and that "the freedom to make, break and reform associations" is a critical feature of the Internet (Brin 2000). Nevertheless, Brin argues that the Internet has "weak mechanisms for filtering good ideas from noise" (Brin 2000). Likewise, social media, from which individuals can upload photos and videos to the Internet, exists (and has arisen since the time of Brin's work) as a vital segment of the same Disputation Arena Brin describes, but may also have weak mechanisms for filtering good ideas from noise. Though this study does not contemplate the actual content of social media messages during the Arab Spring in Egypt, it is interesting to note that, more than a decade after Brin's study, there still does not appear to be a true filter for the noise that exists in the Internet realm.

Certain, recent literature provides a "common understanding of what social media is and how it is utilized by various individuals and groups" (Thompson 2011, 167). The outstanding cultural anthropologist Michael Wesch, a forerunner in social media literature with publications on the subject too numerous to detail here, writes compellingly throughout his work about new media changing "what can be said, how it can be said, who can say it, who can hear it, and what messages will count as information and knowledge" (Wesch 2012). Interestingly, as Robin Thompson points out, "Facebook and Twitter actually welcome and encourage users to support causes for political and/or

---

[15]Many thanks to Dr. Alex Ryan of the School of Advanced Military Studies (SAMS), United States Army, for making me aware of David Brin's outstanding work.

social change" (Thompson 2011, 168). Moreover, Thompson helpfully describes the formula for rallying support to a cause through social media, which actually occurred on a frequent basis throughout the Arab Spring. This formula includes capturing as a video, and posting to a social media application, "an egregious behavior at the hands of a government authority against a presumably innocent person[. This video then] quickly spreads throughout the region via the Internet" (Thompson 2011, 175).

In his 2011 book, *A World of Becoming,* noted political theorist William Connolly discusses new social movements. Within these new movements, social media clearly plays a significant part. It is not hard to understand, for example, Connolly's point that "each antagonistic party in this global (resonance) machine periodically takes action that inflames the others" (Connolly 2011, 139) when discussing events such as that of the Arab Spring. That is to say, protestors exploit social media to their advantage as part of a resonance machine to ensure that the world believes their government is oppressing its people. In a sense, it is the military's response to this—the Egyptian Army's own resonance machine—which this study seeks to examine.

Even military leaders have spoken recently about the importance of social media, and have referred to it as a battlespace (Rendon 2011). The Chief of Staff of the Army (CSA), General Raymond Odierno, recently described the importance of advanced technology, through which "any individual, military or civilian, can alter the trajectory of an operation with the push of a button on a cell phone" (Odierno 2012). Without mentioning the Arab Spring other than to say "the trajectory of the Arab Spring is by no means fixed," it is not hard to imagine the CSA's awareness of the power of individuals with camera phones transforming the nature of military operations in Egypt and beyond (Odierno 2012).

Arab Spring-Specific Social Media Literature

The second main body of literature relevant to this study encompasses the events of the Arab Spring itself. To a large extent, this literature centers on the ability of various social media components, such as Facebook, Twitter, and individual camera phones, to unite and inspire massively popular gatherings. It also describes the importance of military relationships between nations (such as the United States and Egypt) whose militaries train together on a recurring basis. The literature, however, is devoid of any substantive discussion of the important effect of social media on Egyptian Army forces responding to the revolution. Though Gene Sharp's pamphlet on non-violence arguably made a difference in certain aspects of the Arab Spring, it obviously did not contemplate such a movement at the time of its writing in 1993. Works described in this section did, however, specifically consider the events of early 2011 at the time of their writing.

Arab Spring social media scholarship heretofore typically focused on protestors and the aspects of new media most conducive to their ability to organize social movements. For example, in their book, *iPolitics*, Richard Fox and Jennifer Ramos explain that "new media sources and tools provide citizens with new opportunities to express and organize themselves around their political interests" (Fox and Ramos 2012, 3). Fox and Ramos specifically argue that "YouTube, Facebook, and Twitter have been critical organizing tools in the recent citizen protests in Northern Africa and the Middle East" (Fox and Ramos 2012, 2).

Some research focuses on the reach of the Internet throughout the protests, the ability of populations to criticize or praise their leadership, and whether "changes in the information and media environment actually promote democratic ideals" (Fox and Ramos 2012, 9). Other studies address expectations of "citizen participation in government" and whether "new media-driven changes and events" affect these expectations (Fox and Ramos 2012, 18). Still others argue that "social media networks have 'placed new tools and resources in the hands of the political opposition'" (Wheeler and Mintz 2012, 268).

Notwithstanding these efforts, the majority of scholarship contemplating the social media aspect of the 2011 revolutions centers on the narrative that "the Internet and social media are being used in the Arab world to mobilize the masses to demand better governance" (Wheeler and Mintz 2012, 259). With authoritarian regimes, such as that of Hosni Mubarak prior to January 2011 in Egypt, in place, scholars argue that the "tug of war between net-enabled citizens and well-armored states is likely to be a feature of the Middle East for the foreseeable future."[16]

Mind the Gap

In light of social movement theory, general social media studies, and specific Arab Spring social media scholarship, a gap in literature emerges. Specifically, the literature fails to meaningfully discuss the specific effect of social media on Egyptian Army forces in early 2011. For this reason, I arrive at the secondary research question described above—namely, to what extent were Egyptian Army forces affected by how

---

[16]One particularly interesting study asks "who will win this contest?" in the future. Deborah L. Wheeler and Lauren Mintz, "Lessons from Internet Users in Jordan, Egypt, and Kuwait," in Fox and Ramos, *iPolitics: Citizens, Elections, and Governing in the New Media Era* (New York, NY: Cambridge University Press, 2012), 282.

they were portrayed in social media platforms during the Arab Spring/Tahrir Square events of 2011? Most importantly, in response to the primary research question regarding how to think about social media in military operations, I make the case that the prevalence of social media significantly affects the environment—namely, the population—to which militaries must respond and must be considered as a factor in planning for security operations.

The gap at which this chapter arrives is significant and worth careful study. As a related matter, however, it must be noted that a lack of scholarship by military practitioners exacerbates the overall gap described here. With this study's focus on the Egyptian military's perspective of the effects of social media, a final question must be asked—namely, what causes this seeming reluctance by military professionals to engage scholars with anecdotal evidence from actual times of conflict (Perez 2012)? To examine this additional question, it is necessary to briefly recognize the existing literature on the lack of scholarship by military practitioners, as well.

Lack of Military Interaction in Scholarship

The lack of literature from a military perspective on the real-world events of early 2011 is emblematic of the gap in social media coverage during the Arab Spring. Though there may be several causes for this phenomenon,[17] most of which are outside the scope of this paper, the aspects most relevant to this particular project are best viewed through the work of Michael Mosser.

---

[17]For example, security concerns, a lack of time in which to write these accounts, and perhaps even an absence of appreciation from leaders may be viewed as significant reasons for this hesitation on behalf of those individuals who may otherwise be willing to engage in the academic arena.

In his outstanding work "Puzzles versus Problems: The Alleged Disconnect Between Academics and Military Practitioners," Mosser argues that practitioners, unlike scholars, do not have time to spend solving puzzles (Mosser 2009). Rather, practitioners focus their efforts on solving problems. Moreover, the urgent need for practitioners to solve problems on a daily basis, according to Mosser, does not allow for policy-relevant research to occur within the otherwise highly qualified population of service members. Ultimately, Mosser asserts that there is reason for optimism, and offers recommendations for both academics and military practitioners to engage one another (Mosser 2009). He cites leading military schools[18] and other efforts the military is making to attempt to engage in scholarship, particularly in the officer ranks. Most pertinently for purposes of this paper, Mosser argues for the publication of "policy-relevant scholarship." By "policy-relevant scholarship," Mosser means that neither academics nor military practitioners should shy away from making their work policy-relevant, or, as he describes it, "a position where academia should inform practice" (Mosser 2009). This link between scholarship and practice exactly what I seek to achieve through this work, as the experiences learned through the Egyptian Army's response to the Arab Spring should be placed in the academic realm in order for policy makers to understand the impact of events on the ground and to ensure that it informs their future decisions.

Notwithstanding the earlier-cited article written by CSA General Odierno, military practitioners infrequently publish accounts of ongoing or recent events. The Arab Spring is no exception to this general rule. Though perhaps this is changing and the

---

[18]Such as the U.S. Army Command and General Staff College (CGSC) and the School of Advanced Military Studies (SAMS).

CSA's article is the beginning of some sort of new trend, a gap exists between real-world knowledge of military events on the ground and the scholarship typically removed in time and space from those real-world occurrences. Military-specific Arab Spring literature, for example, tends to focus on the importance of existing military-to-military relationships where "contacts between U.S. and Egyptian military officials during the earliest stages of the protest movements in Egypt . . . illustrate the impact of long-standing exchanges and relationship-building" (McKenzie and Packard 2011, 105). Such relationships are especially important due to the massive uprisings which will pose increasing challenges for military leaders called upon to respond peacefully and effectively to such movements. However, this narrow focus ultimately reveals a smaller, though not less significant, gap which this study seeks to lessen.

CHAPTER 3

RESEARCH METHODOLOGY

Given the literature, a descriptive study of events from a military perspective during the Arab Spring appears particularly well-suited to fill the above-described gaps. For this reason, I utilize the oral history of an Egyptian officer who led a company of soldiers throughout several months of intensive security operations in Cairo's Tahrir Square. As such, this study serves as a (small-scale) ethnography of sorts. Yet, in recognition of the fact that a proper ethnography takes years to conduct, the term "descriptive study" remains the most appropriate description for this work.[19]

Regardless of the characterization, this approach takes advantage of the first-hand experience of the Egyptian Army commander with whom I had the good fortune of serving. This unique perspective is largely unavailable to the authors who have written on the subject over the past year. More importantly, the use of a first-hand account mitigates the challenge presented by the recent nature of the events studied, in that it allows for a more thorough and detailed description of actual events than existing—yet incomplete—data sets otherwise would.

This is not a statistical study. Rather, it is a "descriptive study of one particular person/event, [which enables the reader to ascertain] minute and specific details that a statistical study could not" (Wesch 2012). When combined with previous attempts to explain the impact of social media, the story of this particular company commander

---

[19]Put differently, a qualitative analysis seems particularly well suited to this situation, as a quantitative analysis would not work well in a study in which the number of cases studied in depth (N)=1.

enables the reader to arrive at a new concept to help militaries understand the critical need to plan for social media on the battlefield.

While some data exists to explain events from the Egyptian protestors' perspective, and includes studies on the actual number of posts, likes, and members of various Facebook and Twitter pages related to the protests,[20] very little data exists either to explain the military 'side of the story' or to capture the military response to the prevalence of social media on the ostensible battlefield. Again, the first-hand perspective included in this study ameliorates the relative lack of data and/or scholarship on this particular aspect of the protests. Moreover, the perspective of the actual commander on the ground, previously unknown, is invaluable to a particularized explanation of the effects of social media on the Egyptian Army.

As political scientist Ian Shapiro notes, the best methodology for this type of work is to begin "with a problem in the world, . . . [come] to grips with previous attempts that have been made to study it, and then [define] the research task by reference to the value added" (Shapiro 2002, 598). Assembling data in this manner is particularly useful in the instance of the challenges faced by the Egyptian Army during the events of the Arab Spring (i.e. a problem in the world). As chapter 2 revealed, no theory appears to exist to explain the propensity of the Egyptian Army to change its behavior when faced with social media implications in Tahrir Square. Chapter 2 therefore represents an attempt to "come to grips" with previous attempts to study social movement theory, social media

---

[20]Political science conferences over the past year have included papers, presentations, and panels on these subjects too numerous to mention here. For an example of this, see the Midwest Political Science Association (MPSA) and Southern Political Science Association (SPSA) 2012 conference materials, on file with the author.

literature, and Arab Spring scholarship. Thus, the task becomes how to add to existing scholarship an understanding of the Egyptian Army's behavior, or, in the words of Shapiro, how to define the research in terms of the value added.

In order to "add value," and in light of both the advantages and disadvantages of the 'descriptive study,' I build a theoretical framework to understand the situation the Egyptian Army encountered vis-a-vis social media during the Arab Spring. Using this framework to explain the technological impacts on social movements in Egypt enables a greater capability to predict patterns of future outcomes in similar cases. When explained in chapter 4, using specific anecdotes from the Egyptian case study, this ("updated Sharp") framework affords tremendous insight which militaries and other organizations can apply in future transformative events to which they may be asked to respond.

The main strength of the descriptive study is the ability to examine actions through the perspective of an actual company commander on the ground, immersed in actual events. By analyzing this anecdotal evidence through the lens of a useful "social media warfare,"[21] framework, it is possible to arrive at some conclusions on social media's ability to change how individuals and, in particular, national militaries, will behave in similar situations in the future. Additionally, this approach contributes a social media perspective to the ongoing examination of Gene Sharp's "legendary handbook of non-violent resistance" (ISN 2012), on which my framework is based.

Admittedly, a quantitative study with a large data set allows for the replication and more rigorous examination of a study, particularly when compared to the oral history

---

[21]Credit for this concept must be given to Dr. Wesch, who coined it during the course of our discussions regarding this topic.

of one key individual, as is the case in this work. However, the approach of this study is useful for several reasons. First, the individual oral history represents the views of an entire company's worth of soldiers, as the commander is capable of articulating the most important views of the men whom he commanded. Second, working from this lowest level of analysis, the individual allows us to gain insight into similar events, avoiding the common mistake of aggregating data at too high of a level and potentially drawing inaccurate conclusions (Kalyvas 2008). Though "it is rather surprising to observe that micro-level studies may also suffer from overaggregation," (Kalyvas 2008, 404), I do not aggregate here. Instead, I simply utilize the anecdotal evidence from the Egyptian Army's experience in Tahrir Square to move carefully toward an answer to the primary research question.

I begin with an agnostic view of whether individuals' behavior was affected by how they were portrayed in social media and perceived by the public. Again, the descriptive study provides the best way to examine the research question at which chapter 2 arrives. Perhaps most importantly, by using the updated Sharp "social media warfare" framework, I am able to identify the most important phenomenon emerging from the events of the Arab Spring—namely, that the Egyptian Army's response to the prevalence of social media in Tahrir Square is both significant and unprecedented.

In addition to generally updating Sharp's framework to include a social media component, I argue that one of Sharp's "mechanisms for change"[22] occurred in certain, key aspects of the Egyptian Army's response to revolution. The change mechanism must itself be updated to include social media considerations. This particular change

---

[22]See chapter 4, sub-part B, for a complete discussion of this subject.

mechanism—conversion, wherein a government or military becomes "rationally persuaded that resisters' cause is just, [and] . . . come[s] to accept the resisters' aims"[23]—absolutely occurred in the specific social media aspect of the Egyptian Army's response to the revolution. Examining the Egyptian Army historical case study in light of an updated version of this particular aspect of Sharp's work reveals yet another useful lesson for integrating social media into future military operations.

Using the literature described in chapter 2 as background is helpful in that it amplifies the benefits of the descriptive study approach. This is because social media's ability to generally influence how people behave, while described in various studies, does not explain the Egyptian Army's response to the social media presence in Cairo in 2011. Only a participant in Cairo 2011 is capable of fully explaining why, for example, the Egyptian Army decided to allow protestors to literally take photos of themselves on tanks for the world to see on social networking sites.

Before analyzing the study to which the three previous chapters have been leading, one final methodological note is necessary. In order to satisfy terms of human subject study requirements, I personally conducted multiple, formal interviews of this direct participant in events—the Egyptian company commander—with both informed consent of the individual himself and appropriate guidance from the human subject authorities governing the program in which I am enrolled.

---

[23]See chapter 4 for a complete discussion of this occurrence.

CHAPTER 4

ANALYSIS

In its conduct of military security operations during the events of early 2011, the Egyptian Army made several command decisions designed to improve public perception of the military through social media. These decisions, at critical junctures throughout the Egyptian response to crisis, form the basis of a useful theoretical framework for analyzing how to think about social media as a factor in military operations (the primary research question identified in chapter 2). In this chapter, I present this framework based on Gene Sharp's pamphlet, and consider the extent to which social media coverage actually affects soldier behavior during military operations. I update Sharp's mechanisms of change to account for the prevalence of social media not previously incorporated in his work. In turn, this allows for an interesting explanation[24] of the case study findings through the lens of an updated framework. I conclude that militaries will conduct key aspects of security missions differently out of fear for how they may be negatively portrayed by social media.

Most importantly for purposes of this paper, the descriptive study of the Egyptian Army's actions during the Arab Spring answers the research question identified in chapter 2. To be exact, an understanding of the Egyptian Army's Arab Spring response adds one possible approach for decision makers to consider when dealing with the prevalence of social media in the world. This complex world, in which armed conflicts are invariably fought, also includes an understanding of the principles Gene Sharp

---

[24]Specifically, I offer a social media analog ('conversion 2.0'), for use by the military, of one of Sharp's avowed mechanisms for change ('conversion').

discusses. It follows that an examination of the Egyptian response, viewed through the lens of an updated Sharp framework, is a helpful way to think about social media during military operations.

In addition, this study meaningfully informs Arab Spring literature from both a media and military perspective. For this reason, I offer background on the three disparate types of media in Egypt, along with a discussion of recent civil-military history in Egypt, as essential context for the Egyptian Army's decision to follow certain principles in its response to the events of early 2011. Above all, as explained in this chapter, the answer to the central research question derived from the literature review in chapter 2 reveals several insights for the way military leaders think about how to conduct security operations. Specifically, Egypt's concern for the international public's perception of its Army led directly to several critical decisions made in attempt to de-escalate the situation in which the Egyptian Army found itself.[25] These actions represent one approach to tackling the challenges associated with the prevalence of social media in today's world. To best understand this approach, a rich description of these critical social media-influenced decisions, and the reasons for which they were made, follows here.

---

[25]Namely, this 'situation' involved the securing of key areas, including the square in Cairo, along with various cultural sites throughout Egypt. President Mubarak had given the order for the Army to secure these areas, which it did because the police forces essentially dissipated. See sub-part B of this chapter.

<u>The Case Study (Descriptive Study)</u>[26]

A re-description of events in Cairo's Tahrir Square in 2011 enables the

presentation of evidence of a watershed moment in the Arab Spring through the unique

oral history of an Egyptian company commander who led soldiers throughout several

months of intensive security operations. For its part, the Cairo-based portion of the

Egyptian Army seemingly changed its operational approach to this particular mission

when it realized how the events in Tahrir Square might be portrayed in social media.[27]

Therefore, it is necessary to know exactly what occurred in Tahrir Square, from the

perspective of the oral history on which this study is based. This re-description of events

is explained, analyzed, and interpreted using the "social media warfare" framework I

propose in this chapter.

When interviewed, the company commander relayed that social media played a

significant role in how the Egyptian Army dealt with the massive protests in late-January

2011. The overall political objective of the military leadership—ensuring the protection

of the population—led directly to both a desire and need for the Army to not only avoid

negative publicity through social media, but also to take advantage of the power of social

---

[26]Credit for this title and my education on the specific subject of descriptive studies belongs entirely to Dr. Wesch (introduced in chapter 2), whose work in ethnographic studies in general and social media in particular is highly renowned. By presenting evidence in this manner, even an "N=1" can help reveal a "moment of recognition [when readers] realize that the words and insights . . . [apply to] their own stories and lives as well." Michael Wesch, e-mail message to author, 26 April 2012. This is because the concept of militaries dealing in a different way with social media is an insight in and of itself. Wesch.

[27]By a "change" in behavior, I mean something the military would not ordinarily have trained for or planned. For example, it is highly unlikely that any Army would deliberately plan to have its soldiers pose on tanks with protestors, or plan prior to a mission to remove all live ammunition from its weapons.

media to disseminate truthful information about its intentions. There does not appear to have been any organizational dissonance related to this approach, either horizontally or hierarchically (Egyptian Army Officer 2012).

Unified in its approach, the Egyptian Army had to figure out how to best position itself to demonstrate its commitment to protect the population. Perhaps this commitment can generally be characterized as a passive observation of, rather than active engagement with, the vast majority of protestors (King 2012). In terms of media portrayal, the Egyptian Army's leadership understood that, regardless of whether events were accurately depicted, greater audiences within the population might only believe the way these events were described by various senders of the information. To counter this possibility, the Army appeared to ease its strict prohibition against military members speaking with any form of media. The leadership, though not officially, at least tacitly approved the practice of soldiers appearing in media outlets to respond to any falsehoods or erroneous information being disseminated by non-official sources (Egyptian Army Officer 2012).

Another example of the Egyptian Army's counterintuitive approach to the massive protests involves its decision to order all soldiers to remove lethal ammunition from their weapons (i.e. to fire blank rounds only, if at all). In fact, the company commanders, to include the subject of this study, went so far as to collect the ammunition themselves to ensure that no one violated this order (Egyptian Army Officer 2012). This particular decision—extraordinary for a military—largely arose because leaders on the ground felt the population would absolutely believe anything they saw from a camera phone video, Facebook page, or Twitter feed (Egyptian Army Officer 2012). To ensure

31

the Army would not be perceived by the public in a negative light through these same

social media platforms, military leaders knew they could not risk inflaming the emotions

of the potentially volatile crowd (Egyptian Army Officer 2012). Thus, by ensuring that

live rounds were never going to be used, the leaders knew any reports of lethal or hostile

fire on behalf of the Army were false, and could react appropriately if such allegations

were to arise.

Yet another response to the prevalence of social media involved the Army

leadership's approval of soldiers' posing on military equipment with protesters (again,

largely to ensure positive coverage on social networking sites). Though these types of

photos did not occur until Mubarak officially stepped down, and could not include any

glimpses of equipment serial numbers or names, many individuals, including children,

took advantage of this unprecedented opportunity to take (and post on various social

media platforms) photographs on tanks and military vehicles (Egyptian Army Officer

2012). This exception to ordinarily strict policy against such activity engendered

tremendous support for the Army amongst the population and, to a worldwide audience,

made a remarkable difference in the perceptions of the military's response to a

challenging security mission (Egyptian Army Officer 2012).[28]

Two aspects unique to society in Egypt may offer further context in the attempt to

fully understand the Army's approach to events in early 2011. The first of these aspects

---

[28]Though faced with potentially hostile situations in the presence of more than
one million protestors, particularly in the early days of the revolution, military leaders
made another counterintuitive decision. Specifically, the Egyptian Army leadership
decided not to impose a curfew in Cairo's Tahrir Square, in spite of the fact that other
critical infrastructure and popular gathering areas were subject to curfew. This further
engendered support amongst the people, who in many instances had left their homes to
take up permanent residence in the Square. Egyptian Army Officer, 27 March 2012.

involves the three disparate types of media present in Egypt—'government' media, 'special' media, and social media. Television stations comprising government media were, prior to the president's resignation, known as "Mubarak TV" (Egyptian Army Officer 2012). Yet, during the first critical days of the Arab Spring, government media outlets apparently played music and deliberately avoided meaningful coverage of the Tahrir Square uprising (Egyptian Army Officer 2012). While this might not be surprising, given the nature of events in Cairo and throughout Egypt at the time, it may begin to explain the Egyptian Army's decision to utilize social media as a means through which to ensure proper coverage of its response to the crisis.

So-called special media in Egypt includes traditional outlets not owned by the Egyptian government, such as Al Jazeera. Unsurprisingly, during the Arab Spring coverage appeared to vary widely and depended very much upon the particular network providing the coverage (Egyptian Army Officer 2012). Although an analysis of specific coverage by individual special media outlets is outside the scope of this paper, it is important to note that Egyptian government authorities are widely believed to have shut down Al Jazeera's Cairo office, revoked its broadcast license, and confiscated its video cameras, rendering the network incapable of transmission for over ten days in the midst of the revolution (Amnesty International 2011, 21). This treatment of Al Jazeera—and other similar treatment of "independent journalists and reporters [allegedly] singled out for attack" (Amnesty International 2011, 21)—was apparently undertaken in an effort to prevent complete coverage of the protests, and concomitant anti-government messages, from emerging.[29] Again, anecdotes of this nature underscore the significance of social media as an outlet for ensuring proper coverage of virtually all aspects of the crisis.

As the third, and obviously most recent, type of media in Egypt, social media is generally regarded as the primary method by which the majority of individuals communicated to both the nation and world throughout the events leading up to and including the Arab Spring. Though the remainder of this chapter contemplates the importance of this particular form of communication, it is worthwhile to recall that the Egyptian authorities are also believed to have shut down both Internet and mobile phone services for several days at the beginning of the massive protests throughout the country (Amnesty International 2011, 21). Though the lack of mobile coverage affected the Egyptian Army's ability to communicate,[30] these particular outages did not last anywhere near as long as those aforementioned measures taken to degrade special media. For this reason, and in particular because of its ability to reach a wide national and international audience, social media became the primary method of communication for both the protestors and the Egyptian Army throughout the events described in this study.

The second aspect providing context for the Egyptian Army's decision to follow certain principles in its response to revolution derives from certain recent civil-military

---

[29]Note that these allegations are against Egyptian government authorities, and not the Egyptian Army, which, as this paper repeatedly suggests, had to find a way to overcome these constraints to communicate to the people its approach in response to the crisis.

[30]For example, commanders on the ground could not, in many cases, speak directly to higher level commanders who were not in the immediate vicinity while the mobile phone networks were down. Though there were other methods by which to communicate with intermediary staff officers, cellular communications were the only means by which company commanders ordinarily spoke directly to their division commander. Egyptian Army Officer, 16 May 2012.

traditions in Egypt. The first of these traditions involves the Army's "reputation of being an 'army of the people,' [which] proved pivotal during the 2011 uprising, when protesters turned to it for protection and asked soldiers to join their cause" (Amnesty International 2011, 13-14). The high regard in which the Army is held in recent decades in Egypt can be traced to its 1973 war with Israel. Though perhaps a "stylized version of contemporary Egyptian history," the notion that the "heroism of the officers and soldiers of Egypt's military" won the 1973 war and "successfully restore[d] Egypt's collective national honor and ultimately its land" remains true today (Cook 2007, 28). There may also be a respect, or healthy fear, of the military on behalf of the population resulting from the high regard with which the military is held in Egypt (Egyptian Army Officer 2012). Without knowing whether the population agrees entirely with this characterization, it is apparent that the maintenance of some sort of status above the actual government authorities enabled the Army to successfully distinguish itself from those individuals who were targeted for removal and condemnation throughout the revolution.

Another aspect of the civil-military tradition in Egypt is the military officer corps' "limited connection to the day-to-day politics and administration of the state[, which enables the officer corps] to focus its attention on the development of a modern, technologically advanced fighting force" (Cook 2007, 77). [31] The Army, for its part, views itself as being a more professional force than either the Egyptian police or other armies within the region, and also views itself as having very good relations with the people of Egypt (Egyptian Army Officer 2012). Moreover, both the limited political

---

[31] Many thanks to Dr. Donald Connelly of the Command and General Staff College for advice, assistance, and the provision of Steven A. Cook's outstanding book on the subject of civil-military traditions in the Arab world.

connection and increased focus on a technologically advanced force appear to have permitted the Army to succeed in its efforts to credibly and skillfully utilize social media, thereby ensuring the accurate portrayal of its actions. In this way, the civil-military traditions in Egypt may further assist in explaining the success of the Egyptian Army throughout the time period contemplated in this study.

To be sure, not all developments in Cairo were positive. Deaths and injuries within the massive protest did occur (Amnesty International 2011). Yet it appears that criminal elements on horseback caused the majority of chaos, as certain isolated pockets of society sought to cause problems in an attempt to depict a heavy-handed and ineffectual response to the protests (Egyptian Army Officer 2012). It is fair to say that the narrative of the Egyptian Army as an effective and understanding 'army of the people' persevered, however, as the criminal efforts were largely marginalized and not ascribed to the Army itself (Egyptian Army Officer 2012).

Since early 2011, even official sources have increased their presence on various media platforms in Egypt. The Army Facebook page, as part of a Defense Ministry effort, has begun to respond to statements and refute incorrect rumors within hours of their release, when necessary and appropriate (Egyptian Army Officer 2012). This represents a break from the typical approach of Arab leadership throughout the region, which has "tended to see the [I]nternet as a dangerous vehicle of popular insurgency, to be repressed rather than harnessed" (Stein 2011, 1).

The findings of this case study are significant for a number of reasons. The first of these reasons involves the unique approach of the Egyptian Army leadership. In many ways, these leaders became "convinced to let the people do the revolution" (Egyptian

Army Officer 2012). Perhaps unsurprisingly, as a result of this mindset, the population

chanted in favor of the Army once it saw the Army's fair treatment and willingness to

maintain security without unnecessary force (Egyptian Army Officer 2012). Simply put,

decisions described here, such as the removal of lethal ammunition and the portrayal of

protestors on tanks,[32] would not have occurred without the persistent presence of social

media.

Perhaps the Egyptian response is part of a larger shift toward many nations'

armed forces' use of social media. For example, a country very different to Egypt—such

as Israel—appears similarly aware of the ramifications of the social media battle. "Over

the last few years, a growing number of Israeli ministries and other state institutions have

taken up Facebook, Flickr, Twitter and YouTube to disseminate the official line and to

manage Israel's international reputation, particularly during times of military

confrontation" (Stein 2011, 1). As one Israel Defense Forces (IDF) spokesman recently

put it, "[o]ne cell phone camera can harm a regime more than any intelligence operation

can"[33] (Stein 2011, 2) Recent word that the United States Army is using Android

technology to forge an internal network capable of expansive use of smart phones is also

significant (Manning 2012), as are several other United States military social media

efforts outside the scope of this work.

---

[32]Some Egyptian soldiers, out of concern for how they might be portrayed in these outlets, even shielded their faces so as not to be identified. Egyptian Army Officer, 27 March 2012.

[33]One IDF-uploaded video related to Israeli operations in Gaza in 2008-09 has been "watched more than two million times." Rebecca L. Stein, "The Other Wall," http://www.lrb.co.uk/blog/2011/04/19/rebecca.l.stein/the-other-wall/ (accessed 10 May 2012), 1.

Two final, significant aspects of interpretation are related to this project.[34] The first of these involves the development of a new theoretical framework, through which the case study must be viewed. The second aspect is the military practitioners' contribution to literature, addressed in chapter 5. I tackle the first here, as Gene Sharp's pamphlet introduced in chapter 2 allows a more thorough explanation of the case study findings.

"Conversion 2.0": A "Social Media Warfare" Framework

Building a theoretical framework to understand the new concepts introduced here is extremely useful. It is especially important because, through the case study approach, I have "describe[d] with as much detail as possible everything [known]" and, from that, [am] able to "build theoretical models for how to understand the situation" (Wesch 2012). As described in chapter 2, Gene Sharp's 1993 work on nonviolence[35] did not contemplate

---

[34]Other significant aspects of these results involve the difference between social media and mass media influence on a given battlefield, particularly with regard to the sender / receiver directness, and the fact that cell phones can go where CNN or Al Jazeera may not be able to—subjects which must be reserved for future research. Interestingly, while also outside the scope of this paper, two fascinating Army narratives emerged from this study. The first is the fact that the Egyptian Army now has soldiers in its ranks who actually participated in the protests in 2011. The second is the story of a major who, even in uniform, joined the protests while refusing to serve with his unit tasked to respond to the events. This individual gained tremendous notoriety in Egypt, and apparently was court martialed for desertion at one point in time. However, due to his notoriety and an unwillingness to inflame public sentiment, the Army withdrew charges against the individual, who has since returned to his unit. Egyptian Army Officer, 16 May 2012.

[35]Although my citation to Sharp throughout this work is based on a fourth edition published in 2010, the original version was "published in Bangkok in 1993 by the Committee for the Restoration of Democracy in Burma." Gene Sharp, *From Dictatorship to Democracy: A Conceptual Framework for Liberation*, 4th ed. (East Boston, MA: The Albert Einstein Institution, 2010), iv. Neither version contemplates social media.

social media. Thus, an update of Sharp's pamphlet, in light of the considerations social media adds to the traditional concept of warfare, is the best means through which to view the new concepts described above.

A brief amplification of Sharp's work is first necessary. Sharp argues,[36] above all else, that nonviolent resistance is more likely to succeed because "military resistance against dictatorships does not strike them where they are weakest, but rather where they are strongest" (Sharp 2010, 29). Sharp also writes of populations' need to avoid being "atomized [that is, turned into a mass of isolated individuals] unable to work together to achieve freedom, to confide in each other, or even to do much of anything at their own initiative" (Sharp 2010, 3).[37] Social media tools such as Facebook and Twitter profoundly reinforce both of Sharp's exhortations, with masses of seemingly isolated individuals very much able to both avoid military strength and work together, as the Arab Spring clearly demonstrates.

In other words, where "people [were] often too terrified to think seriously of public resistance," (Sharp 2010, 3) experiences such as the Arab Spring illustrate this may no longer be the case. Sharp states that there are "difficulties and dangers in attempts to communicate ideas, news, and resistance instructions while living under dictatorships" (Sharp 2010, 55), yet social media may significantly mitigate these difficulties, as well. Lastly, in the portion of his work in which he describes "dictators [who] are sensitive to actions and ideas that threaten their capacity to do as they like" (Sharp 2010, 19), Sharp

---

[36]See chapter 2 above.

[37]This is highly reminiscent of Hannah Arendt's ground-breaking work on atomization and action arenas in society.

39

engages in a critical discussion of change mechanisms which may appear in a society. I will return to a discussion of these change mechanisms, and an application of them to the Arab Spring events in Egypt, in a moment.

Two important aspects of Sharp's work must at this point briefly be mentioned, as they are directly applicable to the social media realm and my endeavor to "update" his work. First, Sharp argues for the use of several tactics of nonviolent protest under the rubric of "communications with a wider audience" (Sharp 2010, 79). In fact, steps seven through twelve of 198 tactics listed in Sharp's manual are designed for nonviolent protestors to widely disseminate their message. These include tactics such as utilization of radio, television, and leaflets in order to reach greater audiences throughout the world. Applied to this study, it is incontrovertible that the use of social media enables groups to communicate with wider audiences.

Second, Sharp urges the use of social weapons as a means of protest, even before the advent of social media. For example, tactics 174-180 of Sharp's pamphlet include the critical need for nonviolent protestors to use tools of "social intervention" (Sharp 2010, 86). "[T]he [nonviolent] struggle is fought by psychological, social, economic, and political weapons applied by the population and the institutions of the society" (Sharp 2010, 30). Under this rubric, the use of social media by the protestors in Egypt and throughout the Arab Spring seemingly fulfills Sharp's goals of "establishing new social patterns," "alternative social institutions," and "alternative communication system[s]" to effectively challenge dictatorships (Sharp 2010, 86).

Returning to Sharp's change mechanisms, it is necessary to describe the three mechanisms most relevant for our purposes here. First, Sharp speaks of *nonviolent coercion*, where protestors eventually cause their opposition's military forces to "become so unreliable that they no longer simply obey orders to repress resisters" (Sharp 2010, 36). While officer leadership in the Egyptian case ordered its soldiers to no longer repress resisters' attempts to take photographs of their military equipment, no evidence in this study exists to suggest that soldiers disobeyed orders to allow for this type of behavior. In fact, it appears that orders were given (and followed) to engage in conciliatory behavior toward protestors.

A second change mechanism did appear in the events in Egypt, as seen in the police response to the situation. This mechanism, known as *disintegration*, involves a regime "fall[ing] to pieces" through complete mutiny and abandonment by its security forces. Though it appears this occurred with the police in Egypt, it does not appear to have been a complete disintegration of security forces, as the Army maintained control and did not abandon the critical areas it had been tasked to secure.

It is Sharp's third change mechanism, *conversion*, which is most appropriate for purposes of this paper and reflects what actually appears to have taken place in Egypt. Conversion occurs "[w]hen members of the opponent group [in this case, the Army, are] . . . rationally persuaded that the resisters' cause is just, [and] may come to accept the resisters' aims" (Sharp 2010, 35). In light of the discoveries in the company commander's oral history, conversion very much appears to have occurred in the social media aspects described repeatedly throughout this work. As a result, a new version of Sharp's conversion change mechanism, or what I will call 'conversion 2.0,' is highly convincing in its applicability here.

Applying this updated mechanism, a group—namely, the Egyptian Army—responds to the prevalence of social media in a way accepting of the protestors' aims. The Army endeavors to accurately respond to protestors' assertions through the protestors' chosen communication tools of Facebook, Twitter, camera phones, effectively bypassing any mass media platforms. The Army manifests this acceptance by, for example, posing for pictures with protestors and removing lethal ammunition from its weapons, being in effect persuaded by the protestors that to do otherwise would be irrational. Convinced that the protestors' cause may be just, the Army, or at least the portion of the Army in Tahrir Square about which we know empirically, changes its behavior. In this way, the Egyptian Army experiences a form of Sharp's conversion and, in so doing, changes the future of a nation.

When presented with a description of Sharp's mechanisms, the company commander described throughout this work agrees with the notion that a conversion of sorts did occur (Egyptian Army Officer 2012). He suggests, interestingly, that the process in fact began a month earlier, as the citizens of Egypt and the world watched the Tunisian Army deal with a massive popular uprising of its own (Egyptian Army Officer 2012). For the Egyptian Army, the Tunisian Army's experience taught it to be prepared for a similar uprising, and gave it the confidence that it would succeed, since the Egyptian Army considers itself a far superior force to the Tunisians (Egyptian Army Officer 2012). In addition, the rapidly dissipating Egyptian police force's constant challenges taught the

42

Army what not to do, and most assuredly demonstrate that the Egyptian police forces did

not experience a conversion of any sort.[38]

Arriving at Tahrir Square with the experiences of the Tunisian Army and

Egyptian police forces in mind, the Egyptian Army had a strong belief that it would not

fail if it generally identified with the protestors' aims (Egyptian Army Officer 2012). The

Army exemplified this 'micro-conversion' with the counterintuitive, social media-

influenced approach described throughout this work. Though it is worthwhile to ask

whether the Army would have reconsidered its approach had aspects of the approach

backfired, or somehow inflamed emotions on either side, the Egyptian company

commander reports that the Army did not even consider that the approach might fail in

any regard ("if you are defending people, you do not expect them to do anything bad to

you") (Egyptian Army Officer 2012). Perhaps this unwillingness to consider any aspect

of failure in its approach truly exemplifies a Sharp-like conversion on behalf of the

Egyptian Army, particularly in light of the Army's documented willingness to take

measures designed to portray both itself and the protestors positively at all times through

social media.

Again, it is instructive to test the framework by applying it to the Egyptian Army

case on which this study focuses. In so doing, the case study helps to explain the

framework clearly. It also enables the application of the framework to other situations,

while at the same time increasing the ability of others to interpret events that may occur

---

[38]Certainly in contrast to the police, which did not have the numbers, logistics, food, or sleep necessary to sustain several days of security operations in the city of Cairo, the Army's strong logistical base, sufficient numbers, food, and proper amounts of sleep enabled its members to perform at a much higher level than the dissipating police forces. Egyptian Army Officer, 22 May 2012.

in their lives or with their militaries (Wesch 2012). Above all, the case study reinforces the important point that militaries' perception of how they will be portrayed in social media affects how they will behave in situations in the future.

Research Difficulties

The inability to ascertain multiple accounts of the events in Cairo reflects a research difficulty, as addressed in chapter 3. It must also be mentioned that a preference within this study for one individual's specific perspective directly impacts the work. In other words, it is certainly possible that this individual is biased in ways unknown to the author. Bias on behalf of the officer could obviously undermine the ability to draw valid conclusions in this type of work, though I have not detected bias in any substantive way in the course of this study.

Notwithstanding the strengths or weaknesses of this particular study, in the fifth and final chapter I re-visit Michael Mosser's call for both sides of the practitioner / scholar divide to produce "policy-relevant scholarship." In the context of the Egyptian Army's response to the presence of social media during the Arab Spring crisis, I argue that a written account of these events from the military perspective represents exactly the type of "policy-relevant scholarship" military practitioners must be willing to produce in order to inform U.S. policy in a truly meaningful way.

CHAPTER 5

CONCLUSIONS AND RECOMMENDATIONS

This study represents an initial attempt to understand the relationship between

contemporary, extremely powerful social media tools and the military. Though the

general topics discussed in this work—namely, social media and Arab Spring—are

broad, the contribution to scholarship is both specific and narrowly tailored to the

transformative events of the 2011 Facebook-organized uprising in Cairo's Tahrir Square.

The focus on the Egyptian Army highlights a concrete problem in the profession of arms

and contributes to an understanding of military practice in the fascinating arena of social

media. The straightforward posit of this paper is that the Egyptian Army's experience in

2011 demonstrates one example of how militaries may think about social media as a

factor in military operations.

Summary of Study and Its Implications

The citation of key literature in chapter 2 supports the assertion that a gap exists

between accessible coverage of social media during the Arab Spring and the perspective

of the Egyptian Army. The methodology, described in chapter 3, combines the advantage

of a descriptive study with a framework through which to view the study, producing a

mini-ethnography of sorts. In chapter 4, this framework assists in an analysis of the extent

to which social media coverage actually changes soldier behavior during military

operations. The framework—essentially a social media analog to Gene Sharp's oft-cited

work in the realm of nonviolent protest—helps to fill the gap described in chapter 2.

Because literature does not exist in detail to explain the social media phenomenon as an instrument for changing how militaries approach security missions, the updated

"conversion 2.0 framework" is a useful tool through which militaries may examine such

problems. Moreover, direct access to a key individual's oral history provides a

tremendously informative re-description of events in Cairo. It follows that the importance

of this study lies in its ability to answer the central research question of how social media

may be thought of as a factor in military operations. Therefore, perhaps the most useful

way to think about social media in military operations is to examine the Egyptian Army

approach in light of an updated Gene Sharp framework.

Returning to the chapter 2 discussion of military practitioners' willingness to

engage in academic debate, another significant implication of this study emerges.

Namely, an unclassified, inside view of the Egyptian Army's response to social media is

exactly the type of "policy-relevant scholarship" Michael Mosser argues military

members must be willing to produce in order to inform U.S. policy in a truly meaningful

way. Optimistically, this paper symbolizes a willingness on behalf of members of the

military, both as subject and author, to engage in a dialogue with scholars on the most

important issues of today.

Too often military professionals do not approach "in a rigorous way" critical

aspects of the operational environment, of which "social media [is] another factor . . .

[influencing] military's actions" (Perez 2012).[39] Though the prevalence of social media

---

[39]Perhaps this is because military practitioners view "a response to social media as [an Information Operation]" in which they may not be trained or authorized to participate. Gene King, correspondence with author, 21 May 2012. Nevertheless, in a critical effort to mitigate the challenge of this inability to fully engage in scholarship, the Command and General Staff College (CGSC) at Fort Leavenworth, Kansas, recently began an intensive scholars' program for mid-level military officers entitled "Local

outlets, particularly in mass uprisings, is unlikely to be reversed, a rigorous approach by the United States Army is necessary in order to understand social media in areas in which it may be tasked to respond in the future. Such an ability will be important, given the possibility of the United States having to respond to massive protests, and the fact that nations with which the United States is a partner will undoubtedly be required to respond to similar events. In practical terms, it is essential to at least understand and anticipate how a crowd will react during massive uprisings similar to those seen during the Arab Spring.

Recommendations

As described in the "delimitations" section of chapter 1, certain related topics are extremely interesting but outside the scope of this work. For example, it would be useful to examine whether the United States Government's response to the so-called "Occupy Movement" behavior replicated that of the Egyptian Army during the Arab Spring. While some might argue that protests and popular uprisings are matters to which police forces, rather than military forces, must respond, it is absolutely necessary for militaries to be prepared for the possibility of the type of security mission described in this work. At a

---

Dynamics of War" (LDW). This program is an important aspect of the development of military practitioners selected to attend conferences, meet other scholars, and publish scholarly work in an effort to bridge the gap between scholars and practitioners outlined in chapter 2 above. In particular, the project—created and led by one of the U.S. Army's leading active-duty political theorists, Dr. Celestino Perez—"aims to close the foregoing gap by [focusing on] how lethal power / military power must always operate in an environment where others (whether international actors or not) have influence." LTC Celestino Perez, e-mail message to author, 3 May 2012. Put otherwise, efforts such as the LDW project are an initial attempt of military professionals to approach critical aspects of the operational environment in a more rigorous way.

minimum, it is possible to view the Occupy movements and other similar transformative movements in society through the lens of this study's findings and implications.

Another brief note is appropriate here. The findings of the study are insignificant with regard to any Law of War implications of the Egyptian Army's behavior. For this reason, I do not contemplate legal aspects of the overall crisis in this article. Again, while the descriptive study of one person/event is tremendously useful for amplifying the existing social media literature, the same (n=1) approach is less helpful to a thorough understanding of other issues, such as the legal implications. These implications, which in and of themselves may already be the subject of law review articles in the legal field, are certainly worth future study.

Additionally, reconciling the findings of this study with United States doctrine is critical. At a minimum, the capacity of social media must be considered before military forces are assigned to a particular area of the world. This is in spite of the fact that it is "[f]ar from clear . . . how much control [a] state will be able to exert over Facebook and other social media sites" (Stein 2011, 2). Relatedly, a willingness to exploit social media to the military's advantage, instead of waiting for the enemy to do so, is certainly a recommendation of this paper.

Though United States forces likely will not instantly resort to taking photographs with civilians on military equipment during the conduct of security operations, the Egyptian response to popular revolution within its borders nevertheless represents one approach to be examined by U.S. military and civilian leaders. Such an approach is reminiscent of political theorist William Connolly's experiential interaction, in which an approach to a problem in the world is undertaken, various decision makers pause to determine the effects of that approach, and ultimately new approaches are tried in light of lessons learned from the previous approach (Connolly 2011). At a minimum, Connolly's theory is yet another useful construct for militaries to consider as they prepare to deal effectively with the possibility of massive popular movements in the future.

Finally, the Facebook-accelerated uprisings in Egypt and throughout the Arab world in 2011 represent the ability of social media technology to serve as a vehicle for organization, demonstration, and change—all at a rate of speed not previously seen or anticipated. While the causes of transformative movements beginning at the local level are both varied and complex, further research into these areas is critical. Exactly what constitutes the best strategy for dealing with these developments is another matter altogether. Nevertheless, it is the hope of this particular project to contribute to an understanding of how militaries will perform security missions in the near future. In light of these emerging trends, further research into these areas becomes both worthwhile and absolutely essential.

REFERENCE LIST

Amnesty International. 2011. Egypt rises: Killings, detentions and torture in the 25 January revolution. London: Amnesty International Ltd.

Brin, David. 2000. Disputation arenas: Harnessing conflict and competitiveness for society's benefit. *Journal on Dispute Resolution* 15, no. 3 (August). http://www.davidbrin.com/disputation.htm (accessed 4 June 2012).

Connolly, William E. 2011. A world of becoming. Durham, NC: Duke University Press.

Cook, Steven A. 2007. Ruling but not governing. Baltimore, MD: The Johns Hopkins University Press.

Ferguson, Niall. 2011. CGSC Guest Speaker Lecture, U.S. Army Command and General Staff College, Ft. Leavenworth, KS. 16 November.

Fox, Richard L., and Jennifer M. Ramos, eds. 2012. iPolitics: Citizens, elections, and governing in the new media era. New York, NY: Cambridge University Press.

Harr, Eric. 2011. The real truth about social media. Campbell, CA: FastPencil, Inc.

Hsu, Justin S., and Brian C. Low. 2010. The leaderless social movement organization: Unstoppable power or last-ditch effort? Monterey, CA: Naval Postgraduate School.

ICRC.org. Police and security forces. International Committee of the Red Cross (ICRC) Resource Center. http://www.icrc.org/eng/resources/documents/misc/57jq3h.htm (accessed 31 May 2012).

International Relations and Security Network (ISN). ETS Zurich. http://www.isn.ethz.ch/ isn/Digital-Library/Special-Feature/Detail?lng=en&id=137747&contextid 774=137747&contextid775=137746&tabid=1451620996 (accessed 31 May 2012).

Egyptian Army Officer. 2012. Interview by author. Ft. Leavenworth, KS. 27 March, 16 May, and 22 May.

Kalyvas, Stathis N., Ian Shapiro, and Tarek Masoud. 2008. *Order, conflict, and violence.* New York, NY: Cambridge University Press.

Kalyvas, Stathis N. 2008. Promises and pitfalls of an emerging research program: The microdynamics of civil war. In *Order, conflict, and violence,* edited by Kalyvas, Shapiro, and Masoud. New York: Cambridge University Press.

King, Gene. 2012. Correspondence with author. 21 May.

Manning, Patrick. 2012. Army stronger with androids. http://www.foxnews.com/scitech/2012/05/12/army-stronger-with-droids/ (accessed 12 May 2012).

McKenzie, Kenneth F. and Elizabeth C. Packard. 2011. Enduring interests and partnerships: Military-to-military relationships in the Arab Spring. *PRISM* 3, no. 1 (December): 99-106.

Mosser, Michael W. 2009. Puzzles versus problems: The alleged disconnect between academics and military practitioners. The Robert S. Strauss Center Bridging the Gap Series, Paper No. 2, March.

Nixon, Ron. 2011. U.S. groups helped nurture Arab uprisings. *New York Times,* 15 April.

Odierno, Raymond T. 2012. The U.S. Army in a time of transition. *Foreign Affairs* (May/June). http://www.foreignaffairs.com/articles/137423/raymond-t-odierno/the-us-army-in-a-time-of-transition (accessed 31 May 2012).

Perez, Celestino. 2012. E-mail message to author. 3 May.

_____. 2011. The soldier as lethal warrior and cooperative political agent: On the soldier's ethical and political obligations toward the indigenous other. *Armed Forces and Society* (18 August). http://afs.sagepub.com/content/early/2011/08/16/0095327X11418322 (accessed 4 June 2012).

Pool, Ithiel de Sola. 1990. *Technologies without boundaries: On telecommunications in A global age.* Cambridge, MA. Harvard University Press.

Proctor, Patrick E. 2008. Media-enabled insurgency as a revolution in military affairs. Monograph, School of Advanced Military Studies, U.S. Army Command and General Staff College, Ft. Leavenworth, KS.

Putnam, Robert D. 1995. Tuning in, tuning out, the strange disappearance of social capital in America. *P.S.: Political Science and Politics* 28, no. 4 (December): 664-683.

Rendon, John. 2011. CGSC Guest Speaker Lecture, U.S. Army Command and General Staff College, Ft. Leavenworth, KS. 20 September.

Shapiro, Ian. 2002. Problems, methods, and theories in the study of politics: Or, what's wrong with political science and what to do about it. *Political Theory* 30, no. 4 (August): 596-619.

Sharp, Gene. 2010. *From dictatorship to democracy: A conceptual framework for liberation.* 4th ed. East Boston, MA: The Albert Einstein Institution.

Sil, Rudra, and Peter J. Katzenstein. 2010. Analytic eclecticism in the study of world politics: reconfiguring problems and mechanisms across research traditions. *Perspectives on Politics* 8, no. 2 (June): *page*.

Stein, Rebecca L. 2011. The other wall. http://www.lrb.co.uk/blog/2011/04/19/rebecca.l.stein/the-other-wall/ (accessed 10 May 2012).

Szmed, Kenneth A., Jr. 2012. Correspondence with author. 21 May.

Thompson, Robin. 2011. Radicalization and the use of social media. *Journal of Strategic Security* 4, no. 4 (Winter): 167-189.

Wesch, Michael. 2012. E-mail message to author. 26 April.

_____. 2011. It's a 'pull, pull' world. THE Journal.com. http://the journal.com/articles/2011/10/12/Michael-wesch-its-a-pull-pull-world.aspx/ (accessed 4 March 2012).

Wheeler, Deborah L. and Lauren Mintz. 2012. Lessons from internet users in Jordan, Egypt, and Kuwait. In *iPolitics: Citizens, elections, and governing in the new media era*, edited by Fox and Ramos. New York, NY: Cambridge University Press.